Words
OF WISDOM

Words OF WISDOM

Those with wisdom will shine as the brightness of the sky

Book
No. 1

ROY MARTIN

Words of Wisdom

Copyright © 2021 by Roy Martin. All rights reserved.

No part of this publication may be reproduced, stored in a retrieval system or transmitted in any way by any means, electronic, mechanical, photocopy, recording or otherwise without the prior permission of the author except as provided by USA copyright law.

The opinions expressed by the author are not necessarily those of URLink Print and Media.

1603 Capitol Ave., Suite 310 Cheyenne, Wyoming USA 82001
1-888-980-6523 | admin@urlinkpublishing.com

URLink Print and Media is committed to excellence in the publishing industry.

Book design copyright © 2021 by URLink Print and Media. All rights reserved.

Published in the United States of America

Library of Congress Control Number: 2020905081
ISBN 978-1-64367-885-6 (Paperback)
ISBN 978-1-64367-884-9 (Digital)

12.11.20

Introduction

The scripture references are from the King James Version of the bible, with corrections of spelling of Old English words.

The words of wisdom for this book came from various sources; some from the bible, some from the authors personal experiences, some from "Old" sayings that contain a lot of wisdom, and some from insights to the author directly from God.

The words of wisdom in this book are in no particular order, so there are no chapters.

The author suggests that, if possible, you take this book with you so you can read it when you have to wait at the doctor's office, while riding a bus, etc. You may feel inclined to read it more than once.

Obviously, this is not an exhaustive study concerning wisdom. You can do your own research concerning wisdom, and make an appeal to God to provide you with wisdom.

It is understandable that some will disagree with what has been written in this book. The author respects your right to disagree.

1

Wisdom is the principle thing, so get wisdom.
But in your getting, get also understanding.

God's greatest pleasure is to be trusted.

The greatest gift a father can give
his children is to love their mother.

Do not argue about who is right.
Argue about what is right.

God's glory is his goodness.

Part of Jesus' ministry on earth was to
comfort the afflicted and afflict the comfortable.

We do not have to earn God's love, but we
must sow seeds to be blessed with a harvest.

All words are seeds, and every
seed produces after its own kind.

Partial obedience is the same as disobedience.

A compliment is to a woman
what a pay raise is to a man.

There is something about a touch
that is different from everything else.

The spoken word has the power
to build up or tear down.

Fun cannot be used to measure whether
something is good or bad, moral or immoral.

Look before you leap. Still waters
sometime run deep, and there will not always
be someone there to pull you out.

Enemies are just as necessary as friends. They are
the only ones that will tell you if you have bad breath.

God's word is light.

A husband should never stop courting his wife.

Hope deferred makes the heart sick.

Strife will void your prayers. It is better
to suffer an injustice than to get into strife.

Don't try to love God with your feelings. Feelings
are too fragile. Love God with your obedience.

We should always honor our fathers
and mothers, even though they are not
always perfect fathers and mothers.

All of God's followers have a promised land.

Substance and honor are in the house of wisdom.

All who hate wisdom love death.

Reprove a scorner and he will hate you.
Reprove a wise man and he will love you.

Our fear of God is the beginning of wisdom.

By wisdom the years of our life will be increased.

Funerals are not for the benefit of the dead, they are for the benefit of the living.

God removes our repented sins from us as far as the east is from the west.

In many counselors, there is safety.

A borrower is a servant of the lender.

Don't take something that is only a part of life and make it as though it is all of life. If you do, your life will be out of balance.

There is only one benefit to being poor. A poor man does not have to worry about being kidnapped and held for ransom.

A man that guards his words guards his life.

Pride and contention are twin brothers.

He that walks with the wise becomes wise.

A good man leaves an inheritance for his children's children. A good inheritance is more than just money and property.

A father that does not discipline
his son does not love him.

Those who are right in their
own eyes are self-righteous.

A soft answer turns away wrath.

Pride leads to heartache, and
eventually to destruction.

Pleasant words are as a honeycomb,
sweet to the soul and health to the bones.

Signs and wonders were the hallmark of
the church when it was first established.

Jesus did not preach a comfortable
religion during his earthly ministry.

The mark of our character is how
we handle correction. Everyone needs to
be corrected from time to time.

Beauty is only skin deep.

You cannot embarrass anyone
who does not have pride.

If man was just another animal, he could not laugh or cry and would not have a conscience.

Love people more than things.

The strength of Satan is due to our ignorance of God's strength in us.

Our authority in the spirit realm is exercised through our voice.

The devil has power, but he does not have authority except what we grant him.

A fool that keeps his mouth shut will be reckoned as wise.

Death and life are in the power of the tongue.

It is an honor for a man to cease from strife.

As a man thinks in his heart so is he.

Being filled is not the same as being fulfilled.

Through wisdom a house is built.
By understanding, it is established.

A loud blessing too early in the
morning sounds more like a curse.

Iron sharpens iron, so a man can be
sharpened by the counsel of a friend.

A wicked man will hear footsteps behind him
even when no one is there. But a wise man whose
heart is right with God will be bold as a lion.

The prayer of a proud man will not
get any higher than the ceiling.

A bribe will blind the eyes of a sincere counselor.

Husbands, treat your wife like a thoroughbred
and she will never become an old nag.

All rivers run into the sea, but
the sea never overflows.

All things have a day of reckoning. Write that in
the concrete walkway that leads to your front door.

What you can walk away from ,
you have mastered. What you cannot
walk away from has mastered you.

Honoring God requires substance as well as words. That substance is the proof of our honor.

Our money is us. When we give money, we are giving a portion of ourselves.

Consider the ways of the ant to be wise. Without a guide, overseer or ruler, he gathers food for the winter.

Refusal to forgive is like drinking poison and expecting it to kill your opponent.

Ask God to love someone through you, then fasten your seatbelt.

If you have to tell people you are humble in order for them to know, then you probably are not.

Pride has a short fuse.

Husbands, if you neglect your wife, holy matrimony will descend into unholy acrimony.

Fathers, hug your daughters. Then she will not be overwhelmed when a man with an ulterior motive hugs her.

Wisdom believes God's promise: if my
people, who are called by my name, will humble
themselves, pray, seek my face, and turn from
their wicked ways; then I will hear from heaven,
forgive their sins, and heal their land.

Fathers, correct your children when they
disobey, but never put them under condemnation.

God did not promise the Israelites a land flowing
with pasteurized, homogenized, skim milk and
artificial sweeteners. This is man impersonating God.

God is more interested in your relationship
with him than he is in your religion.

If all of the violin players in an orchestra
tune up on the lead violin player, then they will
all be in tune with each other. So, it is with us and
God, who is the chief musician. Those that are in
tune with God, will be in tune with each other.

Parents, use a paddle or switch to
spank your children, never use your hands.
Hands are to be used for loving.

A perfect husband is one who does not expect his wife to be perfect. A perfect wife is one who does not expect her husband to be perfect.

To please God, never stop being a student where his word is concerned.

Time is the currency of relationships, including our relationship with God. So, allocate a certain part of your day to spend with God and his written word.

Wise men sought Jesus. Wise men still seek Jesus.

Whosoever finds God, finds life.

God will hold us accountable for even the idle words that we speak.

You cannot conquer what you refuse to confront.

Grudges that you nurse will continue to get bigger, just like a baby that is nursed.

Jesus commanded his followers not to leave home without the Holy Spirit.

To see into your future, add 20 years to your present age and see yourself there.

Our anointing with the Holy Spirit will
glorify God if we demonstrate God's power.

Religion is comfortable because
we don't have to prove anything.

Chasing after fun is like chasing after the wind.

Your parents can teach you how to work,
but they cannot teach you to like work.

People will be held accountable to believe
the gospel if they see it demonstrated.

If you were accused of being a servant of God
before an unrighteous judge, how would you plead?

Don't play church like little girls
play house. Be the church.

The word "lord" means owner. A
landlord is the one who owns the land.
If Jesus is your lord, he owns you.

Every drop of blood that Jesus shed for
us is important. So, don't waste any of it.

Be on God's side, and he will be on your side.

Waiting to accept Jesus as your savior could be risky. Noah did not wait until it started raining before he started building the Ark.

God has commanded us to forgive so we can live in a world that is not fair.

If you fear death, anyone who holds the threat of death over your head will be your master.

The one who qualifies to be the head of the household is the one who is willing to be the last one out if the house catches on fire.

The integrity of the message is dependent upon the integrity of the messenger.

A successful marriage is a two-way street concerning love.

It is better to be rebuked by God than to be praised by Satan.

Faith in God requires patience. When patience ends, faith ends.

Abortion sheds innocent blood. Those that don't know this are devoid of wisdom.

Do not despise a thief if the
only thing he steals is food.

Men, treat wisdom like a sister.

To be wise, hate what God hates: pride,
lying, hands that shed innocent blood, wicked
imaginations, feet that runs after mischief, a
false witness, and he who sows seeds of strife.

Wisdom is better than diamonds or rubies,
and nothing else can be compared to wisdom.

Before the earth was, wisdom was.

Wisdom loves those who love her.
Those who seek her early will find her.

Exalt wisdom. It will bring
honor and promote you.

Who or what you honor will
determine the course of your life.

God does not do anything but talk. He rules and
creates by words. He created us in such a way as to be
able to hear his voice, so he can instruct us. Then we
repeat the words we hear, which will transport us from
the kingdom of darkness into the kingdom of light.

2

If we acquire God's wisdom, we will leave this world differently. We will go out with joy. We will be led forth in peace. The mountains and the hills will break forth before us into singing, and all the trees of the field will clap their hands.

The bible say God's word is wisdom, so put as much of God's word in you as you can.

The wisdom that is from God toward us by the way of his Spirit is called "fruit". It is love, joy, peace, patience, kindness, goodness, faith, gentleness and self-control.

A nation can enlarge its wealth, but that does not mean they have increased their joy.

Words of Wisdom

Let us ask God for wisdom, so
that we can number our days.

We call our property on earth after
our own name, believing this will somehow
cause us to live forever here on earth.

All roads lead to the cemetery.

Wisdom is answered prayer for those
who are in the valley of decision.

Without a clear vision, a nation will perish.

God's wisdom says that in a
marriage, one plus one equals one.

Hell has no back door.

God is a promise keeper.

You will know you don't have wisdom
when you wake up some morning and realize
that most of your future is behind you.

God's wisdom says, "If you will be willing and
obedient to God, you will eat the good of the land."

Wisdom is the womb where revelation
is developed. Understanding is where
revelation takes its first breath.

We usually do not fall into sin. We ooze into it.

If you need more wisdom, ask God. But
ask in faith, believing you will receive.

Nip evil while it is in the bud stage.
If you wait until it is fully grown, it will
be much more difficult to uproot.

We cannot overcome evil thoughts with right
thoughts. We overcome evil thoughts with the
right words, even if the words are spoken under
our breath. Memorize Second Corinthians 10:5.

God said, "Before you call, I will answer." He
did not say, "I will answer even if you don't call."

The good shepherd will see to it that
his sheep will lie down in green pasture;
not brown, drought-stricken pasture.

God does not just have the answer for our
problems, he is the answer for our problems.

Dying is not the worst thing that can
happen to us. Dying with regrets of not having
lived a purposeful life is much worse.

Where your treasure is, is
where your heart will be.

Giving to God from the heart causes God
to bless us in whatever we put our hands to do.

Develop a grateful heart, even for small favors.

Meditation brings revelation. Revelation brings
manifestation if we have intimacy with Jesus.

God's word is truth. Without knowing
the truth, we can never be truly free.

Your biggest audience is you. You look at
yourself more than anyone else looks at you.

He who is faithful in what is least,
is also faithful in what is much.

Controlling your mouth will
help protect you from the pit.

To please God serve him from a position
of faith, not from a position of fear.

Self-condemnation will void
God's blessings for your life.

Man-made righteousness will never please God.
Remember the Tower of Babel. (Genesis 11:4-9)

God's mercies are new every morning,
because we need them every day.

Forgiving others is not a one-time thing.

Praise the Lord when you feel like it.
Praise the Lord when you don't feel like it.
Praise the Lord until you do feel like it.

A big shot is a little shot that kept shooting.
The bible talks a lot about persistence.

A completed work is a portrait of the one who
did the work, so autograph your work with excellence.

You may have the power to speak as you
please, but you don't have the power to determine
the consequences of what you speak.

If the bible says God's mercies are new every morning, then God's grace must be also, because grace and mercy are God's goodness.

If the Lord is your shepherd, what does that make you? The Lord has committed himself to provide for his sheep.

Exercise caution when you put your life in the hands of professionals. Remember, it was professionals that built the unsinkable Titanic.

Jesus' wisdom in feeding 5,000 people shows us how to multiply by dividing.

People look mostly at the outside of people, but God looks on the heart.

Our worship of God can also be used as a weapon against demonic forces.

Our praises towards our God will cause a shift in the atmosphere around us in our favor, because God inhabits the praises of his people.

In the consummation of all things, God will shake both the heavens and the earth.

The only thing that will be left standing will be those things that cannot be shaken.

The wisdom from Jesus says to take up your own cross daily and nail to it everything in your life that needs to die: the pride, grudges, bitterness, fears, hate, etc.

Not everyone likes to clean house, but everyone likes a clean house.

Delight yourself in God, and he will crown you with loving kindness and tender mercies that you can use towards others.

Like the members of the new church in the book of Acts, Christians need to pray for boldness.

If anyone says to you, "There is no such thing as absolute truth." You reply, "Are you absolutely sure about that?"

Life is mostly influenced by decisions. Postponing a decision is a decision in itself.

God has obligated himself to bless his servants.

How hard would it be to be a friend
with someone who is exactly like you?

Jesus said that those who hear and do
what he says are wise. Notice the word "do".

Don't corrupt your wisdom for the
sake of your pride or fleshly cravings.

It is all right to be as wise as a serpent
as long as you are innocent as a dove.

The road to hell is paved with good intentions.

It is better to suffer persecution in the world
due to our obedience to God than to suffer in
hell forever due to our disobedience to God.

Hell is not necessarily for
people that you don't like.

If you are not prepared to die without
fear, you are not prepared to live a fulfilled
life, because death is a part of life.

Listen to God's wisdom: I know the
thoughts that I think toward you. If you seek
me with your whole heart, you will find me.

College is where we learn how to learn.

Pride tends to major in minors.

Your knowledge is in proportion to how much you read. Your useable knowledge is in proportion to what you read.

When Jesus was on the earth, he was persecuted because he demonstrated the kingdom of God, so will we be persecuted if we demonstrate the kingdom of God.

If you feel more comfortable with the baby Jesus than you do with the adult Jesus, it is because the baby Jesus doesn't talk back.

Pessimists will look at a half glass of their favorite beverage and says, "it is already half gone." Optimists will look at it and say, "It is still half full."

The time to take pie is when pie is being served. If you wait until you are ready for it, it may all be gone.

We don't know where the wind comes from or where it goes, but we can hear it and see the results of its power. So it is with the Spirit of God.

What we focus on continually, whether good or bad, will gradually overpower us; so always be aware of where you are projecting your focus.

Being willing to demonstrate the kingdom of God is essential if we want to represent God to an unbelieving world.

God loves you just the way you are. He loves you enough not to leave you the way you are.

God has committed himself to bless those that diligently seek him. Notice the word "diligently".

Don't be afraid to take an honest to goodness look at your own responsibilities in your relationship with God. Seek a personal, close experience with him. This is in addition to your knowledge of the scriptures.

God is a giver. To qualify for his gifts, we must be also givers. Our first gift is giving ourselves to God. All of our other gifts flow out of this.

Don't give the devil a ride. If you do, it will not be long until he will be doing the driving. He will take you to some places you don't want to go, and keep you longer than you want to stay.

Being almost saved is the
same as being totally lost.

The bible says, "Don't let your left hand
know what your right hand is doing." What does
this mean? Don't let the part of you that doubts
know what the part of you that believes is doing.
When you tithe with your right hand, don't let
your left hand know what you are doing.

When a good shepherd notices one of his
sheep is missing, he searches until he finds it.

What does the bible mean when it says a
wayward son "came to himself"? It means the
son was going through a humbling experience
because he wasted all his resources.

Do not be surprised if God does not ask you
for your opinion about anything. But he can still
be touched by the feelings of your infirmities.

The bible says, "Multitudes, multitudes
are in the valley of decision, for the day of the
Lord is near in the valley of decision."

Trust God that he has your best interests at heart.

Jesus said that he came to earth to
serve, not to be served. The bible charges
us to have the same mind set as Jesus.

The conflict of the ages is who is going to be
the boss; whether it is in a nation, in a church, in
a school system, in a work place, or in a home.

We rob God of his glory when
we fail to tell others of the good things
we have experienced with him.

A discussion extolling God's power lacks
credibility if God's power is not demonstrated.

Married couples, you should show your
spouse more love than you show your cat or dog.

God made man in his own image. Man
tries to make God in his own image.

Broad is the road that leads to
destruction. Narrow is the road that leads
to eternal life, only a few will find it.

Racism travels a two-way street.

As a servant of God, you have the authority to rebuke every tongue that arises against you in condemnation. No weapon formed against you will prosper.

For those whose heart is "right" before God, death will not be a hurtful experience. It will be like falling asleep.

Being a teacher or preacher is an awesome responsibility. The number of people you can help is the same number you can hurt.

It takes at least two parties to make peace, but it only takes one to make war. Regardless of how much you want peace, if the other wants war, there will be war.

To bear big fruit, you will need big roots.

Experiencing good success might cause you to let your guard down and not see the pit up ahead.

Pride is a manipulator.

Fools despise wisdom and instructions.

Prosperity does not destroy
everyone, just the fools.

Trust in God with all of your heart. Do not
depend solely on your own understanding.

Happy is the person that finds wisdom
and understanding. When you lie down, you
will not be afraid and sleep will be sweet.

Put away from you the disobedient mouth.

Applause is intoxicating. Don't seek it,
unless you want to become intoxicated.

Wisdom is like gravy. You take some for
yourself, then pass it on to the next person.

Sticks and stones can break your bones,
but only words can break your spirit.

Go easy on your doctor. Remember,
he is only practicing medicine.

How would you respond if someone
said to you, "What are you living for?"

3

You can fool some people all the time. You can fool all people some of the time. But you cannot fool all of the people all of the time.

Songs can sometimes contain great words of wisdom: I will rain upon your desert says the Lord. I will pour my spirit out right where you hurt. I want to be your confidant and friend, because my love for you will never, ever end.

When God asks someone to do something, he never asks them if it is convenient for them to do what he asks them to do.

Those who cannot find time for physical exercise, will need to find time for illness.

A joyful heart is good medicine, but a
broken heart makes the bones feel dry.

There is a story in the bible of a man who had
two sons. One was lost in a foreign country, and
the other was lost in his own backyard. Which of
these two can you identify with? (Luke 15:11-32)

Those who live by the sword,
will die by the sword.

If you look up to you, you will
probably look down on others.

Forgiving others even if you don't feel
like it, does not make you a hypocrite. God
requires us to forgive. The bible says the wisdom
that is from above is without hypocrisy.

When the cat is away, the mice
will play. How does this relate to our
believing that God is always with us?

If God appeared to you in a dream, like he
did Solomon, and said he would grant to you
whatever you asked for, what would you ask for?

Our world has an abundance of things that should make people feel satisfied, so why are there so many who are dissatisfied?

It is not wise to bad-mouth someone who is holding a gun on you.

Husbands and wives, if you want to stay close to each other, keep God's word between you.

It is not always the size of the dog in the fight that determines the outcome, sometimes it is the size of the fight that it is in the dog.

Jesus said he came to serve, not to be served. Does that mean he desires to be our servant?

We tend to elevate knowledge but neglect experience, especially an experience with God.

If you do not tell someone the truth, you do not love them. If someone does not tell you the truth, they do not love you.

We need to take care of our planet. As far as I can tell, it is the only one that has chocolate.

God gives people the freedom to make their own
decisions, even when those decisions have unfavorable
consequences. God did not make us robots.

The bible admonishes us to search for wisdom as
we would for money or hidden treasure. The bible says
the place to start searching for wisdom is God's mouth.

We can talk about Jesus, sing about Jesus, preach
about Jesus and most people will not get offended;
but when we imitate Jesus by healing the sick, casting
out demons and raising the dead, we will definitely
be persecuted just like Jesus was persecuted.

A riddle will sometimes contain wisdom.
According to the bible, Jesus is a physician,
yet he did not spend his time practicing
medicine the way physicians do.

A rose by any other name is still a
rose. A lie by any other name is still a lie. A
skunk by any other name is still a skunk. The
shedding of innocent blood by any other name
is still the shedding of innocent blood.

Do not try to convict sinners of their
sins. That is the Holy Spirits job. If you do it,

the Holy Spirit will be unemployed. Do you
want the Holy Spirit to be unemployed?

No one else can speak your mind for you.
Every rooster has to do his own crowing.

The riddle of all riddles: Can God bless a
nation that blesses the shedding of innocent blood?

Our first revelation of true love will be
when we truly believe that God truly loves us.

Would it surprise you to know that God
loves everyone equally? However, you have to
accept God as your father to reap his blessings.

If you are reading your bible and do
not understand a certain passage, it would
be wise to ask God to explain it.

Perfect love is not our love for God, but God's
love for us, which can be perfected in us by God.

When we wake up each morning, it would be
wise to say to ourselves, "God loves me." Or sing,
"Jesus loves me this I know for the bible tells me so."

It may be wise to ask yourself, "Is my God my belly?" Remember Esau. He traded his birthright for a bowl of stew.

We will need to be persistent when battling demonic spirits, because they are persistent.

Time will erase your beauty.

We must have power from on high to carry out God's command to go into every man's world and demonstrate the gospel.

Most people want to be saved, but some do not want to be saved from their sins.

Man's wisdom pales alongside God's wisdom.

Abraham Lincoln was criticized because he never joined a church. Here is his response, "Churches have so many different creeds it is confusing. If I ever find a church whose only creed is to love the Lord thy God with all thy heart, all thy mind and all thy soul; that church I will join with all my heart, all my mind and all my soul."

Our sins cost Jesus his life.

God loves our offenders as much as he loves us.

Pray for those despitefully use you, or
speak all manner of evil against you.

Our God is a heart God.

Our God is great and is greatly to be
praised. Even the ocean roars with his praise.

How we respond to trouble will
usually determine the outcome.

Public acceptance of something
cannot overcome our private rejection.

Unload your load on Jesus. He can handle it.

If you want your prayers answered,
be an answer to someone's prayer.

Whenever you do someone a favor who is having
a bad day, the effect of your favor is multiplied.

Judgement begins in the house
of God, according to the bible.

There is a special type of love that is supernatural. God uses this type of love when he bestows special favors on those that serve him, who acknowledge God as their father in the face of an unbelieving world, not just in church or at home.

If our relationship with God is strong, we can still find an area where we can serve him even if we are not in perfect physical health.

The peace that Jesus offers us is not necessarily the absence of war. The type of peace Jesus offers, we can have while we are fighting a war.

Intimacy allows for honesty.

It is all right to question God as long as we do not have any preconceived ideas as to how he will answer.

Whether the storm is inside your life or outside your life, it has to obey your words spoken in faith in Jesus' name.

The roads we travel in life will not always be paved, sometimes they will not even be gravelled.

God likes what his children like if it is within the boundary of scripture.

Do not be subject to worry, God is
still on his throne. If he falls off his throne,
then you need to start worrying.

Jesus said to his followers, "Nothing shall by any
means hurt you." Nothing includes death, it will not
be a hurtful experience, it will be like going to sleep.

In serving God, accept the fact that his
instructions may seem illogical. He told Joshua
to march around Jericho seven times and the
walls would fall down when everyone shouted.

If you do not yet love God, at least trust him.

Praise the Lord in the beauty of his holiness.

In relationships, a beautiful personality
is more important than a beautiful face.

There are gods, then there is God.

God cannot help you if you will not let
him help you. Say to God every morning,
"I trust you to help me today. I trust you
to help me keep my head on straight."

If you are obviously over-weight, don't worry about how your hair looks.

The most misunderstood word in the English language is probably the word "love". It is not our fault. Other languages such as Greek, have different words for the various types of love. Some types are based on emotions. Some are based on an act of our will, or will power.

Let the peace of God be your umpire when deciding if something is godly or ungodly.

Bad experiences can sometimes produce something good if we learn something from those experiences.

Sometimes pushing people to do something is like pushing a string.

How can wisdom help you if you refuse to embrace it?

As we age, we should be able to acquire more wisdom.

The kingdom of God is not something we can see, but we can see the end results of it. If we cannot, then it is just religion and not the kingdom of God.

The kingdom of God can be in the world, but it is not a worldly kingdom.

You will know that you are in the kingdom of God when the kingdom of God is in you.

Preaching the kingdom of God takes priority over the preaching of a funeral, according to the bible.

To the degree that you are impacted by the kingdom of God will be the same degree that you are transformed.

Wisdom is having the correct knowledge concerning the kingdom of God, and understanding is knowing how to use the knowledge.

The kingdom of God is the power of God in the word of God and in the Spirit of God to empower the children of God to do the works of God. (to get the full impact of what this is saying, read it very slowly)

Listen to the wisdom of Jesus, "Come unto me if you are heavy laden, and I will give you rest." How do we come into Jesus, with words?

> If you could explain a miracle,
> it would not be a miracle.

Man's wisdom says, "Wherever there is a will, there is a way." Jesus' wisdom says, "I am the way."

Allow God to share his holy nature with you.

> Prayer towards God has the
> power to reveal you to you.

4

It is not wise to measure ourselves by ourselves
or compare ourselves to ourselves.

The power that a thankful heart will have
over your life will change you for the better.

We come unto God with our
words. Our words are our life.

In olden days, God's people believed; therefore,
they spoke. We believe; therefore, we speak. If we
don't speak, that is proof that we don't believe.

A friendship or a marriage will be broken
if you cannot control your mouth.

When you are dealing with a broken
heart, talk to your heart; tell it to beat again.

Sometimes we have to make a choice between
satisfying our flesh or satisfying our soul.

Life does not have a rewind button,
but it does have a restart button.

In the physical world, we claim things with
our hands. In the spiritual world, we claim things
with our tongue; we speak what we want to claim.

The bible says we will be more blessed when we
give than when we receive. So, look for ways to help
others with your time, your talents and your money.

We will take on the nature of the one
we believe, either God or Satan. This is what
happened to Eve in the Garden of Eden.

Our relationship with God and Jesus
could be and should be our highest priority.

The bible says the one thing that
is needed the most is to sit at Jesus' feet
and listen to what he has to say.

We cannot stand afar off and expect God
to hear our voice, because we cannot make
our voice sound like thunder. Come closer
to God, and he will come closer to you.

Other people hearing God's voice does not help
us develop our own personal relationship with God.

How can we develop a deep relationship
with anyone if we never talk to them, or talk
only occasionally? So, it is with us and God.

A dollar saved is worth more than a dollar earned,
because you don't pay taxes on the dollar you save.

Do not call things as they are if you want to
change them. Call them according to what you want
them to be. If God called things as they are, the earth
would have continued to be void and without form.

Let the weak and the poor and the
fool and the sick say, "I am strong. I am
blessed, I am wise. I am in good health."

Let the wise aged say, "God satisfies my
mouth with good words. My youth is renewed
like the eagle." If you don't believe this, say
it over and over until you do believe it.

Jesus knocks on the door of your heart with his voice, not his knuckles. So, listen for his voice.

Jesus said he is the light of the world. Those that don't believe this will walk in darkness. He was referring to the light of life, not daylight.

If we will judge ourselves, we will not need to be judged by God.

Jesus said he came to earth to seek and to save those that are lost. When he left the earth, he passed that job on to his followers.

God is not opposed to us having money. He is opposed to money having us.

A person with an experience is never at the mercy of a person with an argument.

Our love and compassion toward people will help them heal a multitude of pain. It will bind up the broken hearted, and set at liberty those that life has bruised.

In the Old Testament, the word "grace" was translated from a root word that means "to bow over by someone toward another who is inferior". When we realize that the God of the universe voluntarily bows toward us to show us favor, we will realize just how amazing God's amazing grace really is.

Jesus taught that those who exalt themselves will be humbled, and those who humble themselves will be exalted.

We have only one life to live. So, we need to make the most of it. We need to do the most good we can, to the most people we can, in the most ways that we can.

Acquiring faith is a full-time job if we expect our faith to be functional and full-time.

When dealing with people, you learn what an asset patience really is; both your patience and their patience.

Faith will push us to do what we normally would not do.

Faithlessness says, "I will believe it when I can see it." Seeing it first does not require faith.

Everything that glitters is not gold.

Divine health is better than a divine miracle
of healing after you have lost your health.

God's blessings for us are voice activated, and the
voice has to be our voice in order for the blessing to
come to us. Speak what you want, and avoid speaking
what you don't want. If you want good health, don't
talk sickness. Even idle words will work against you.

Sometimes we limit God by our limited thinking.

It is better to have God's wisdom than
man's wisdom. However, we can have both.

The more time we spend talking to God and
reading his word, the more wisdom we will have.
Wisdom may come gradually, but it will come.

If you are not sure how to handle a
situation, ask God; then exercise patience
while waiting for the answer.

It would be wise to exercise caution when
judging God's motive for doing whatever he does.

Having a thankful heart has to
be practiced, which involves looking
beyond your own personal world.

Don't wait until someone dies to start seeing things about them that you are thankful for.

Do not be conformed to the way the world thinks, but be transformed by the renewing of your mind to what is good, and acceptable, and perfect in God's sight.

By your patience, you will possess your soul.

There is a certain amount of mystery about God. The more we know about Jesus, the more we will know about God. So, study the scriptures that tell about Jesus' earthly ministry.

The good in your life that you are not thankful for, you are apt to lose.

Is it the culture of your life to fix everybody or a culture of being thankful?

If someone asks you, "What is missing in your life?" How would you respond? Would you say, "I am not as thankful as I should be?"

When we don't practice being thankful, we set ourselves up to be deceived by Satan, the master deceiver.

The opposite of being thankful is being selfish.

The bible says to enter into God's gates with thanksgiving and into his courts with praise (which is also a form of thanksgiving).

When we practice being thankful, faith is moving toward us. When we don't practice being thankful, faith is moving away from us.

Could it be that more marriages would be blessed if each one practiced being thankful? Say it. Write it. Show it. Demonstrate it.

A sense of lack could come from being unthankful.

How would your personal acquaintances respond if someone asked them if you are a thankful person?

If married couples would keep thankfulness in their marriages, their marriage will grow and glow.

If you find it difficult being thankful, look for at least one person each day to whom you can show a favor. This will cause a shift in your mood toward being thankful.

You can have perfect conduct and character if you write your own bible, and some do.

Pride is a stench in the nostrils of God. The bible says God hates pride.

People need to learn how to disagree without becoming disagreeable. They need to learn how to disagree in a way that does not cause the disagreement to escalate into animosity.

The regrets of your past do not dictate your future unless you allow it to do so.

God's word is spiritual food. We are spirit beings. Our spirit requires spiritual food in order to have vitality.

He that guards his mouth, guards his life.

Jesus is the High Priest of our confession if we confess him.

There is a difference between "truth" and "facts". Facts are subject to change. Truth is eternal. God's word is truth. Truth spoken can change facts, but facts cannot change truth.

There is a difference between "reading" and "meditating". Before Joshua fought the battle of Jericho, God said to him, "Meditate on my word day and night". God did not say, "Read my word day and night". Could this instruction apply to us when we have battles to fight?

The currency of heaven is faith. With it we can acquire whatever we need.

Having Jesus guide your life is like having power steering in your car.

Saving someone from the fires of hell is somewhat like trying to save someone from a burning house who does not know that the house is on fire. We tell them their house is on fire, and they say, "I don't smell any smoke."

A borrower is a servant to the lender, according to the bible.

Wisdom is a tree of life for those that embrace her, according to the bible.

The bible says God scorns the scorners, but gives grace to the lowly.

The wise will incur God's glory.

Many hands make work small.

An unruly tongue is like the spark
that started a great forest fire.

The wise learn from their experiences. But
the wisest learn from other people's experiences.

The bad things people do are apt to be
remembered longer than the good things they
do, especially after multiple generations, unless
we engrave the good things on stone.

It is more difficult to tame the tongue
than it is to tame a wild animal.

Developing a grateful heart has to be
practiced. No one is born with a grateful heart.

The word "blessed" in the bible was
translated from a word that actually means
"supremely blessed", which indicates it
comes from someone who is supreme.

Horse sense is what is keeping a
horse from betting on a man.

In marriage we select a mate based on looks. We enter into a marriage based on a vow. We live out a marriage based on our feelings. Is it any wonder why there are so many unhappy married people?

There is nothing wrong with wanting to be like God. We should be the most concerned when we don't want to be like him.

Wise people sometimes change their minds. Fools resist changing their minds.

God's word is so important that he has elevated his word above his name. It makes sense, because if our word is no good our name is no good.

God's word is wisdom, according to the bible.

God's word is our rear guard.

God's word is a shield against sin.

God's word is the expression of his nature, and the measure of his character.

God's word is God.

God's word is the kingdom of
God, according to the bible.

God's word is seed. When he speaks into
the world, his seed will produce a harvest, and
prosper in whatever place he plants it.

A lazy man will not cook the game he
got while hunting, according to the bible.

A virtuous woman is a crown to her husband.

A man shall be commended according
to his wisdom, the bible says.

The wicked are snared by the
wickedness of their own words.

A fool is always right in his own eyes.

A heavy heart will cause us to stoop.

Poverty and shame will go to a person who
refuses instructions, who refuses to be corrected.

The rich have many friends, but
they may not be true friends.

> He that is slow to get angry
> is of great understanding.

Could it be that King David was a man after God's own heart because he continually expressed thankfulness for what God had done? He certainly was not perfect in his conduct. Reading his writings may help us develop a thankful heart.

Listen to the wisdom of God, "I am God, and there is none like me, declaring the end from the beginning." (note: Being able to declare the end from the beginning is proof that he is God.)

The righteous have hope, even in death.

A wholesome tongue is a tree of life, according to the bible.

When we are humble, we have to be on guard that we don't become proud of our humility.

The bible referring to the devil as a snake does not mean he was one. He was like a snake in that he was sly, and cunning, and subtle, and fascinating. Fascinating? Yes, fascinating. Eve must have found him to be fascinating. She had never seen him before, yet she believed him rather than God.

Pride trusts in man's wisdom.

Pride is a trap that even the wise might fall into, because pride can blind our eyes to the trap.

How do we pursue wisdom? We pursue it diligently and on purpose.

God will make you face what you fear the most, so you can become fearless. However, he will be with you all the way.

There is nothing wrong with a boy wanting to be like his father, even his heavenly father.

Do not forsake mercy and truth. Write these words on the tablet of your heart.

In all your ways acknowledge God, and he will direct your steps.

Do not resist the chastening by God. Those God loves, he chastens, according to the bible.

Happy is the one who finds
wisdom and understanding.

Those who have wisdom and understanding
will walk safely. They will not stumble.

Don't withhold from those in need if
it is within your power to help them.

Be on guard against the little things
that can spoil your day. Remember, even
little foxes can damage the vineyard.

If you do not want to get your feet
wet, never walk close to the edge of a lake.
This is wisdom for any area of your life.

Let your eyes look straight on. Turn not
to the right hand or to the left hand. This
will protect you from many sorrows.

Our expectancy is huge with God. If
you don't expect him to do what he says
concerning you, he probably won't.

Sometimes life teaches us something that
we did not want to learn in the first place.

The mark of a great leader is not only how he handles responsibilities, but also how he handles privileges and success.

Wearing a cross would be like wearing a hangman's noose if we don't know why Jesus died on the cross rather than by some other means. It freed us from the curse, because the bible says, "Cursed is everyone who hangs on a tree." Some places in the scriptures refer to the cross as a tree.

We align with God when we learn the will of God, when we do the will of God, when we become what God wills us to become.

How good and pleasant it is for the people of God when they worship in unity. This opens the door for the Holy Spirit to come into the church like a mighty, rushing wind.

To read and meditate on the scripture we must discipline our minds not to wander and discipline our bodies not to be lazy.

Spiritual armor and a spiritual weapon are essential for doing battle with a spiritual enemy.

Independence and individualism will work against us if we have committed ourselves to serve God.

Our viewpoint of the spiritual realm is only a view from a point, the point where we are. We must seek counsel from others who have a different viewpoint. When we have many viewpoints, we are safer on the battlefield.

A kingdom without spiritual power cannot be successful when attacking Satan's kingdom.

Satan has power, and he is not shy about using it.

To do battle with a spiritual enemy, we must be willing to get out beyond our comfort zone.

The primary purpose for miracles is to demonstrate God's divine power and glory, even though they benefit us also.

We must allow God to speak to us. This will require patient listening rather than demanding formulas.

There are five kings in our lives that we want to rule over us: Sight, Hearing, Smell, Taste,

Touch. If you don't see these as kings, it is because you are being deceived by the master deceiver.

The kingdom of God cannot be inherited from our ancestors.

If you have committed your life to God, would it surprise you to know that God thinks of you as one of his jewels?

God honors our obedience, not our intelligence.

We take our focus off of God when we take our focus off of his word, because God's word is God, according to the bible. If you want more of God in you, put more of his word in you.

Pride will sometimes tell more than it knows.

The bible says God feeds the birds, but it does not say he throws their food into their nests.

It appears from the bible that God will allow his servants to be sorely tested in order for them to gain battlefield experience.

The bible says God is longsuffering.
So, when we partake of longsuffering,
we partake of the nature of God.

Do not meditate on anger or strife.

God's love never fails, but there will
be times when we fail to walk in it.

Be patient in perfecting God's love in
you. Change takes time. Old ways die hard.

When we walk in God's love, we walk in peace;
because God's love perfected in us casts out fear.

Love is not rude or selfish.

The bible says Jesus is made unto us wisdom,
righteousness, sanctification and redemption.
When we have Jesus, we have it all.

Prayer to God is an act of worship,
an acknowledgement of God's sovereignty
and his role as our spiritual father.

The degree of our humility toward God
determines the limits of our usefulness to God.

Pride is slow to listen and quick to speak.

Pride can cause us to believe we
have faith in God when we don't.

Pride has no sense of guilt
when it makes others wait.

Pride believes it is humble.

God knows the proud, but
he knows them from afar.

Pride is similar to faith. Sometimes it is
difficult to tell the difference. Our pride will
sometimes masquerade as faith in God.

Timidity is not humility. We
have to work at being humble.

Pride is Satan's counterfeit of faith.

Humility is our protection
against Satan's deceptions.

God hates pride. If we could see it the
way God sees it, we would hate it also.

Pride gives the prideful a rush, a thrill
of pleasure in their minds and emotions.

Pride will try to manipulate
the pride that is in others.

Pride believes it can worship God in its own way.

Pride hurries others, but does
not want to be hurried.

Pride wants to be the boss, but
resents being bossed, even by God.

Pride does not believe it can be deceived by Satan.

Pride believes humility is
weakness, even cowardly.

Pride will often answer a
question with a question.

Pride will sometimes answer a question
directed toward someone else.

Pride believes pride is the same as honor.

Pride accuses others of being insensitive
when it does not get what is wants.

Pride is a wisdom killer.

Pride and contention are constant companions.

Pride will suffer physical pain if
necessary in order to continue in pride.

If you accidentally stray from God,
stay humble and he will bring you back.

If you do not like being bossed,
you will not like God.

God referred to Moses as "Moses my
servant". Substitute your name for Moses
in that statement and see how you feel.

In order for us to become a new creature
in Christ, we have to reckon our present
nature as being dead, graveyard dead.

A prideful person will have difficulty
remembering even one sin in their life. This is one
way to determine if you are a prideful person.

If it is out of sight, it is probably out of your mind. So, if you want to take something with you, leave it where you can see it.

Men, if you want to get married and you expect God to help you find a suitable wife, don't show him four pages of the traits you want in a wife. If God found a girl with all of those traits, he might decide to marry her himself.

Many times the most important thing in life is a question. Life would be boring without questions.

Every problem we face in life is an open door for more wisdom.

What is your reaction to a problem? This could reveal to you what your destiny is or is not.

Do not be overly concerned if you understand only 10% of what you read in the bible. Ten percent of something is better than 100% of nothing, and nothing is what you will have if you don't read the bible. Just be obedient to the ten percent that you do understand, and in due time God will give you more understanding.

There are many ways to acquire
wisdom, but there are two ways that are
very effective: mistakes and pain.

One of the purposes for learning is
to bring about a change in your life.

According to the bible, one of the
ways we learn is by beholding (seeing).

We are transformed supernaturally by
beholding. A man named Peter saw Jesus walking
on water. Peter was transformed into the same
nature as Jesus, then he walked on water, also.
When he stopped beholding Jesus, he began to
sink. How does this relate to our problems in life?
Can we walk on problems if we behold Jesus?

We have to know what the bible says
in order to do what the bible says.

The bible says the Lord's blessing is like dew
upon the grass. What does this mean? Dew is water.
In a country receiving a limited amount of rain,
like Israel, this is the water the grass depended
upon to grow and flourish. Plants can absorb
water through the leaves as well as the roots.

God's grace is the antidote for
the curses that came upon mankind,
beginning in the Garden of Eden.

The kingdom of God is mentioned
129 times in the bible, so it must be very
important for us to know what it involves.

The gospel is also referred to in the bible
as the gospel of the kingdom. So, anyone who
preaches the gospel must also preach the kingdom,
or else the gospel will not be fully preached.

6

Use discretion in burning bridges when running from hurtful relationships. You may need to cross back over those bridges in order to mend those broken relationships.

The bible says God's goodness is demonstrated by his grace and mercy.

A coward dies a thousand deaths, but the brave die only once.

God's truth offends some people, especially those that do not want to make the changes that are necessary to conform to the truth.

The truth never needs to apologize. But we need to apologize if we do not speak the truth in love.

What is truth? Truth is a person, his name is Jesus. Truth is God's word. The truth became flesh and dwelled among us, the bible says.

The Holy Spirit is referred to in the bible as the Spirit of Truth. If you want to know the truth about yourself, talk to the Holy Spirit. He is your counselor.

Obedience to God is better than our sacrifice to God, according to the bible.

Sometimes the old church hymns contain a lot of wisdom: Trust and obey, for there is no other way to be happy in Jesus, but to trust and obey.

Time used properly is like a fruit-bearing tree, which does have a season.

Exercise patience, or else time will become your enemy.

We honor God when we resist our disobedience toward God.

What does the bible mean when it says to fear God? Jesus contrasted this with fearing Satan. Jesus said the most Satan can do is kill you, but God can cast you into hell, which Satan cannot do.

The bible says to honor the king and
fear God. Do not get these two reversed.

We cannot discipline a demon, and we cannot
cast out our flesh. But we can discipline our flesh,
and cast out a demon. We must do both of these.

According to the bible, hell and destruction
are never satisfied, never fulfilled.

Money and property can be inherited,
but respect has to be earned.

Can a man rob God? God says his servants
can. How? By withholding the tithe.

A doctor who performs an abortion has innocent
blood in his hands. God hates the hands that shed
innocent blood, according to the bible. Notice that
God does not hate the person, just the hands. So,
there is hope for the doctor if the doctor will repent.

Your church does not define who you are,
whether denominational or non-denominational.
On judgment day, God will not say, "Well done,
thou good and faithful Methodist or Baptist
or Catholic, etc." You hope to hear God say,
"Well done, thou good and faithful servant."

Fellowshipping with God is a pure treasure.

Pray for your enemies, if you do not, and they die in their sins, their blood will be upon your head, according to the bible.

There is no such thing as a white lie or a black lie or a fib. A lie is a lie, is a lie.

There is no such thing as a partial anointing.

There is such a thing as a neglected anointing. King Saul was anointed, but neglected to do what the prophet told him to do.

There is such a thing as a misused anointing. The prophet Balaam was anointed, but he put himself up for hire.

There is such a thing as an abused anointing. King David was anointed, but he shed the innocent blood of Bathsheba's husband.

Some people believe the tithe is part of the curse that Jesus' crucifixion delivered us from, but they do not believe the Ten Commandments are part of the curse, although both are part of the Old Testament.

Is there any tangible evidence that someone is "saved" as prescribed by the bible? What if they forgave those that they formerly refused to forgive?

Jesus only washed the feet of his servants. If he was on the earth today, would he wash your feet?

There is a common belief that all people are God's children. That is not what Jesus taught. His said the religious leaders of his day who opposed him were children of Satan. He never referred to them as his brothers.

Jesus said those that continue in his word will know the truth, and the truth will make them free. Notice the word "continue", that tells us this scripture is about a journey, not a one time event.

Those who have a covenant with God have covenant rights, one of which is to be free of demonic oppression. However, this is not automatic. You have to rebuke demons in Jesus' name.

There are some things that will come to those that are in covenant with God that they will not have to struggle for or fight for. But there are other things that we have to contend for, we will have to fight for them because we have an adversary who steals, destroys, and even kills to prevent us from having those things that God promises in his covenant with us.

You do not have to live with a broken heart. That is good news. That is the gospel.

Lazy people usually despise those who are not lazy.

Most people want their lives to be better, but many do not want to do what they need to do to make it better.

Say to God every morning when you arise, "I promise to serve you today." Or. If you are musically inclined sing, "Oh, Jesus, Lord and Savior. I give myself to thee, for thou in thine atonement did give thyself for me. I own no other master. My heart shall be thy throne. My life I give, henceforth to live, oh Christ for thee alone."

Life can only be lived one day at a time. However, we can still analyze the past and plan for the future.

If you do not know the purpose for something, you are apt to misuse it and maybe abuse it. This applies to our personal life as well as our relationships, such as marriage. If you do not know the purpose for marriage, you are apt to misuse or abuse it.

A beautiful face will gain your attention, but it will not endear you to people's hearts.

Hunger and thirst are not limited to food and water. We can hunger and thirst for conversation, for music, for intimacy, etc. The bible says, "Taste and see that the Lord is good."

Sometimes we would like to have a comforter, a helper, a counselor. God's Spirit is all of these. It would be wise to invite him into your life.

Would this be an accurate interpretation of the words and wisdom of God? "I did not make you a chicken. I made you an eagle, so you can soar above the troubles of this world."

If you believe your mission in life is to fix everybody, don't be surprised if people don't enjoy your company.

Parking yourself in a church pew every Sunday does not make you a disciple of Jesus any more than parking yourself in a garage makes you an automobile.

Do not discount a small beginning. It may lead to bigger things. The largest river in the world has a beginning so small that you can step across it. Great faith sometimes begins as small faith.

If you attempt something for God but fall flat on your face, do not get discouraged. It would be wise to pick yourself up, dust yourself off, and go at it again.

If you run from the devil, that is not victory, that is defeat. Hit him with a sword. The sword of the Spirit, which is the word of God. Not just any word of God, but the words that plead the blood that Jesus shed when he died to deliver us from the devil. You can be sure the devil knows about that blood.

People do not need to learn how to diet. They need to learn how to eat. Dieting seldom solves a long-term problem.

Those who are wise will shine as the brightness of the sky, according to the bible.

Our God is a patient God. However, he will come suddenly to judge the earth; or we could die suddenly, and would not have another chance to accept the salvation that Jesus offers.

In the spirit realm everything can hear,
both physical and spiritual entities. This is
why Jesus could calm the storm and cause
a fig tree to die, just because he spoke.

When God opens a door, no one can shut
it. When God shuts a door, no one can open it.
Could this be the reason God shut the door of
the Ark, so Noah could not open it when the
flood came and his kinfolks wanted to get in?

If you pray for your enemies, God will
bless them. The blessing could prompt them to
repent just like it caused a sinful fisherman to
repent when God filled his boat with fish.

Here is how not to pray for patience,
"Lord, give me patience, and give it to me right
now." If you pray this way, you might hear the
Lord say, "I will give it to you tomorrow."

The biggest little word in the English
language is probably the word "if". As you read
the bible, notice the impact that it has.

The heart of a wise man will
teach his mouth what to speak.

A whisper campaign against someone
can cause as much hurt as a fist.

Dealing with a fool and his foolishness
is like dealing with a mother bear that
has been robbed of her cubs.

Rewarding evil will cause it to continue.

An offended brother is harder to be won
over than a strong city can be won in a battle.

A man who wants friends should
show himself to be friendly.

There is a big difference between being
convicted and being condemned. It is good to be
convicted, because it can bring about a conversion, a
transformation from darkness to light. Condemnation
will not do this. This is why Jesus told the woman
caught in adultery, "Neither do I condemn you."
Then he spoke words that obviously indicates
he convicted her, "Go and sin no more."

The right words connect us with God,
and connect people with each other. The
wrong words disconnect us from God, and
disconnect people with each other.

God blessed Abraham so he would not only
be blessed himself, but be a blessing to others.
Since God does not show favoritism, this would
also apply to God's other servants. How can
we bless others if we are not blessed ourselves?
You cannot give what you do not have.

You can learn more by listening than
you can by talking. Depend on wisdom to
tell you when to talk and when to listen.

If you have fallen down due to life's heavy load,
don't expect Satan to feel sorry for you. He will hit
you while you are down. He does not fight fair.

Satan knows the power of words. He is a
master with words. He can speak all languages.
He knows how to use the words of the bible
against you. He is also a musician, and he will
use the songs of his servants to deceive you.

To be God's servant, we have to commit ourselves
to do what he says. Whether we want it or not.

There is nothing like food to bring people
together. It would be wise for a family to eat one
meal together each week away from home.

The family cook needs an occasional break from the daily routine of cooking. If they don't get it, you might walk into the kitchen someday and see a sign posted that says, "This kitchen is closed due to illness. I am sick of cooking."

When Satan tries to tempt you, he may use scripture from the bible, just like he did when he tried to tempt Jesus during his earthly ministry.

Sometimes, haste makes waste.

If you have a dysfunctional family, for whatever reason, pray for all of you at least one time each day. Pray, "Thank you Lord for healing our family." Then say prophetically, "We are blessed. We are wise. We are in good health."

Fame can bring you temporary pleasure, but it will not bring you happiness, it will not prevent you from feeling lonely.

Sometimes nightmares are dressed up like fairy tales. The bible says wolves will dress themselves up to look like sheep.

When you live in selfishness, you live in a very small world.

There is no substitute for reading the bible for yourself. Reading books about the bible may help you understand the bible, but should always be compared to what the bible says about itself.

A really good leader will donate some of his time to help others to be really good leaders.

Parents, be cautious about giving your children unearned money and "participation" trophies, rather than earned money and "achievement" trophies. Which one of these resembles the real world in which your children are destined to live?

Mental assent is not the same as faith.

Handled properly, money can help us create some good experiences with people. Handled improperly, money can help us create some enemies.

7

Hear the wisdom of God, "I know the plans I have for you, plans to prosper you and not to harm you, plans to give you hope and a future."

There is a difference between the world's wisdom and God's wisdom. Man can make great gain knowing the world's wisdom, but will never know God using the world's wisdom.

The bible could be interpreted to mean that God assigned to the father of the family the task of disciplining the children of the family. One of the reasons that God chose Abraham to be the father of many nations is because he would "command" his children (Gen. 18:19). The bible could be interpreted to mean the mother of the family is to nurture the children and be the "glue" that holds the family together. Unfortunately, some single mothers may not believe they can fill the role of the father, so the children may not receive adequate discipline to deal with a troubled world.

God does not want his children to grieve alone. If you cannot find a family member or church member to grieve with you, ask God to grieve with you. When grieving has served its purpose, God will set you in a large place, according to the bible.

If you are a servant of God, he has promised to contend with those who contend with you.

Are you brave enough to ask God to let you see you as he sees you?

A good marriage begins with an obedient mouth. A good marriage continues to be a good marriage due to an obedient mouth.

Being embarrassed in the eyes of the public doing something that God wants you to do is a small price to pay to be obedient.

Married couples take a vow to love each other as long as they live, not as long as they feel like it (you don't need a vow for that).

Jesus' command to forgive others is a
command, not a suggestion or recommendation.

The bible says "Deep calls unto deep".
What does this mean? Something deep within
God (his Spirit) is calling unto something
that is deep within us (our spirit).

You never outgrow your need for a hug.

God has promised to be a father to the fatherless.
So, take heart if you don't have an earthly father that
claims you or does not take an interest in you.

If you are in right standing with God, no
weapon formed against you will prosper. Every
tongue that arises against you in judgment, you can
condemn. This is your heritage as a servant of God.

God's voice is light for those who hear his voice.
When you stop listening, the light will go out for you.

One of the devil's most powerful weapon's is a
question. So, beware! He said to Eve, "Did God really
say...?" He said to Jesus, "If you are the son of God..."

Salvation is free to us, but it is
not cheap. It cost Jesus his life.

We sometimes miss something in life because we don't ask for it, or strive for it, or fight for it.

God does not always come as soon as we call him, but if we have set our love upon him, he has obligated himself to answer our call. However, he did not say he would answer immediately, or in what way he would answer us.

We say what we believe, and we believe what we say. It is not enough to just believe in God's word, we have to say what we believe in order to establish it in our heart permanently.

Hatred has its pleasures, but pleasures in the flesh. Love for God has its pleasures, which the bible calls "joy", and it is in our spirit.

Being merciful without a conviction for doing so can be risky, because there will usually be someone who is merciless who will oppose you.

What is an occult? It is the other person's religion, not my religion.

When we do not practice a thankful heart, we open the door of our innermost council for Satan to enter in.

When you are angry, the only side you can see is your side, unless you have been practicing being thankful.

Without God's help there is no way you can win against Satan. He is smarter than you, and more powerful than you.

Be wary of people who offer council without knowledge.

Success is not granted to anyone, it has to be earned. However, God's grace to us is a gift.

Fake wisdom will try to hide behind humor: When you come to a fork in the road, take it.

Men who cannot get along with their mother-in-law should remember King Solomon, who had 700 mothers-in-law. How much wisdom would be needed by Solomon.

God must surely have the heart of a teacher. He gives tests with multiple choices. He sets before us "life and death" and asks us to choose one. But he is also a benevolent teacher, because he tells is the best one to choose is "life".

Unless God builds the house,
those that build it labor in vain.

Out of the abundance of the heart, the mouth speaks. If you want to know what someone has in his heart in abundance, listen to them talk. They may be able to cover up for a while, but if they talk long enough they will reveal what is in their heart in abundance.

Sometimes the biggest problem in serving God is not having to deal with Satan, but having to deal with time. Abraham and Sarah waited ten years for the son to be born to them that God had promised.

Whoever loves the most can be hurt the most, this includes the Holy Spirit. It might be the reason that speaking against the Holy Spirit is the only sin that cannot be forgiven.

There once was a man who complained because he had no shoes, then he met a man who had no feet.

The prophet of olden days continually reminded the people that though God sometimes tarries, he will always show up on time, on his time.

When you hear a voice telling you
to do something good but you don't want
to do it, the voice is probably God.

Faith in God is not in our head but in
our heart. Our heart refers to the core of our
being, not to the organ that pumps blood.

The root word from which the Hebrew
word "shalom" comes, means "nothing missing,
nothing broken". When nothing is missing and
nothing is broken, we have peace (shalom).

The bible says it is better to be poor
and have integrity than to be rich and be a
fool that is perverse with his mouth.

Whosoever is deceived by
strong drink is not wise.

There is gold and there are rubies, but words of
knowledge are the most precious jewels of all jewels.

Do not seek the company of someone
who flatters with their words.

The bible says the spirit of man is the candle
of the Lord, who searches all of the inward parts.

Train up a child in a way he should go,
and then when he is old he will not depart
from it. However, in between young and
old, he may have periods of rebellion.

In some cultures the core of our being is referred
to as the "heart", in some cultures it is the "kidney",
in some cultures it is the "liver". A boy would say
to his sweetheart "I love you with all my liver."

The bible says it is the goodness of God that
leads people to repentance. But this requires time
and effort on our part to read and meditate on the
part of the bible that reveals God's goodness.

Wisdom is to our soul what honey is to our body.

Here is the wisdom of God to his prophets in
olden days, "Write the vision plainly on a tablet,
so that those who read it can run with it."

To worship anything or anybody other
than God is the same as worshipping Satan.

God knows our bodies, he remembers that
we are made from dirt. Dirt cannot worship God.
God is a spirit, and those who want to worship him
must worship him in spirit and in truth. The words

we speak in worship must come from our spirit
even though our bodies give voice to the words.

The mercies of God are from everlasting
to everlasting, and his righteousness unto
children's children; to those who remember
his commandments to do them.

Whatever bothers your conscience needs to be
fixed, whether sin or something else, whether big or
small. Ask God to help you if you need help. You
cannot receive the abundant life that Jesus promised
if something weighs heavily on your conscience.

During his earthly ministry, Jesus told his
followers that they would do greater works than
he did. What does this mean? His followers would
testify of the power of salvation for their lost
souls, of which Jesus could not testify because
he was never lost. Getting people saved through
our testimony is the greatest of all works, because
salvation is the greatest of all miracles (works).

God touches those who touch
him through worship.

Our grace and peace are multiplied
by our knowledge of the scriptures.

How can you know when you have really committed your worries to God? It is when you refuse to allow the worries to come back into your mind. The worries will try to come back. Speak to your worries, "Worries, I have committed you to God, and I refuse to accept you back." You may have to say this 20 times a day for awhile, but it will lessen as time goes by. Rest assured that God will show up when he sees that your commitment is firm, and will remove your worries. When he does, don't forget to thank him for it.

Addiction is not always a bad thing. It depends on who or what you are addicted to. It is good to be addicted to God and his word. God's word is God.

Daily bread from God requires daily contact with God, in Jesus' name. Jesus referred to himself as bread, and he referred to his miracles as bread.

Release those who owe you an apology. Mark their debt PAID IN FULL. Jesus paid everyone's debt on the cross. Refusing to release those who owe you an apology is a state of rebellion.

Humility will draw God toward you.
Pride will push God away from you.

When you confessed your sins was not when God first found out about your sins. That was when you got free of them.

Forever is a long time. Hell is not the place you want to be when you find out just how long forever is. It is wiser to believe there is a hell, and find out later there is not a hell, than to believe there is not a hell, and find out later there is a hell. If you are risking an error in your thinking, always error on the side of safety.

Check your motive for doing whatever you do. You might learn some things about yourself of which you were not aware.

God said in the bible, "Whosoever finds me finds life." We would be practicing wisdom if we believed that.

Your surrender to God must be unconditional.

8

It does not require much wisdom to know that whatever we sow determines that we will reap. We cannot sow wheat and expect to reap barley. The bible uses this analogy concerning the speaking of words. The kind of word we speak (sow) determines what we will reap. So, choose your words carefully. If you sow discord, you will reap discord, etc.

When trying to reach inside a person, appeal to their sensibility, not to their depravity. Instead of scolding a rebel, say, "I believe you could do better if you really tried."

The safest place to be is in the middle of God's will.

Jesus told his followers, "If you are meek like me, you find rest for your soul."

Without wisdom, things can be perverted. Does a woman have a right to privacy when she wants to shed innocent blood by aborting her baby?

One of the consequences for refusing to forgive those who wrong you is that you are not liberated.

There is a risk that comes with a blessing. You could become selfish or you could become lazy.

It is not wise to believe that God controls everything and everybody, because the bible does not teach that. Read the bible carefully and see for yourself.

The bible says the kingdom of God is at hand is the same as saying God's spirit is available to all who will invite God into their life.

There are times in everyone's life when we will have to make life-altering decisions, destiny decisions. We not only need information but also revelation. It would be wise to ask God for help.

Always keep Jesus between you and God. When you foul things up and God looks toward you, he sees only Jesus.

The day will come when knowledge of God's glory will cover the earth, as the waters cover the sea.

Some people do not believe that Satan exists, that the name is just symbolic of evil. If what the bible says about Satan is inaccurate, the entire bible loses credibility. It would be wise to believe what the bible says about Satan.

We cannot claim wisdom if we are ignorant of the fact that Satan is a master deceiver.

If we will obey God, he has promised in the bible that blessings will come upon us and overtake us. We will be the head and not the tail (those are God's words).

The bible does not say that money is the root of all evil. It says the love of money is the root of all evil. The rich are not the only ones who love money.

Satan knows how to use your fears against you. God's perfected love in you will cast out fear.

No one can serve two masters. You cannot serve both God and yourself, unless your desires are the same as his desires.

We brought nothing with us when we came into this world, and we most assuredly will take nothing with us when we go out.

Would it not be wise to assume that God will overlook our imperfect knowledge of him if our heart is perfect in our desire to know him?

If you want to be wise and qualify for God's blessings, including eternal life, say to God, "My commitment to you is solid. From now on you are number one in my life."

We start life longing for physical pleasures. We end our life longing for spiritual pleasures.

Love God forever, live forever. This type of love involves an act of our will, not our emotions. It is the type of love God uses to love all the people of the world.

Pride is a powerful motivator, but in the wrong direction.

If someone calls you an ugly name, you reply "I don't care what you call me as long as you don't call me too late for supper."

When God tells you to do something,
make it a priority in your life.

Confidence in an unfaithful person during a
time of trouble is like having a foot out of joint.

The bible says seeking our own glory has
the same effect as eating too much honey.

Many people are more interested in
talking about religion that they are in talking
about God and his plan for their life.

What do you do when your dream becomes
a nightmare? Not the dream while you sleep,
but the dream for your future. Would it not be
wise to let God help you select your future?

How can two walk together unless they
are in agreement? The Holy Spirit did not come
until Jesus' followers were of one accord.

As a dog returns to his vomit, so
a fool returns to his foolishness.

A lazy man is wiser in his own conceit
than seven men who can render him advice.

As a man who shoots flaming arrows,
so is the man who deceives his neighbor
then says, "I was only joking."

When there is no more wood the fire goes out,
so where there is no tale bearer the strife ceases.

The words of a slanderer cause
wounds deep in the belly.

What right do you have to criticize the work of another man's employee? Only on his employer does he stand or fall. What right do you have to criticize God's servant in his work toward God? Only on God does he stand or fall.

Anger can cause hurt, but so can envy.

Even honey is not attractive to a man
with a full belly, but to those who are really
hungry even sour food tastes good.

Be wary of the devil. He is like a roaring lion, seeking someone to devour. A roaring lion is a hungry lion. A lion with his belly full does not roar, he sleeps.

A hearty counsel from a trusted friend
is like a sweet smelling perfume.

Whoever cares for a fruit tree is entitles
to eat of its fruit. So it is in all of life.

A greedy person is like a blood sucking
horseleech, a flat worm that has a mouth
on each end. You can almost hear the leech
say. "Give me blood. Give me blood."

Wisdom is sometimes difficult to understand.
The locusts have no king, yet they go forth like a
mighty army with a king. And spiders can be found
in the palace of a wise king, according to the bible.

You do not seek praise from others. The
task that you do well will praise you.

If you have something people want,
don't be surprised if they show up at your
house at an inopportune time, or telephone
you at any hour of the day or night.

Trust God to show you the way
home, your heavenly home.

If you are not ashamed to associate your name
with God, he will gladly associate his name with you.

King Solomon wrote that where there is much wisdom, there is much grief; and to increase in knowledge, is to increase in sorrow. He wrote these words towards the end of his life. When searching the scriptures concerning his life, we see he filled his life with what satisfied his flesh and emotions, and neglected his inner man, his spirit. Let us not make the same error, and neglect our spirit.

A man can have much wisdom and a little folly, yet he will be more apt to be remembered for his folly than for his wisdom.

Telling only half of what you know concerning a serious situation is the same as telling a lie.

Sometimes wisdom does not appear to be wisdom. It took God less than a year to get the Israelites out of Egypt, but it took him 40 years to get Egypt out of the Israelites.

We can be both humble and adamant. It all depends upon the circumstances and the type of person we are dealing with. We need wisdom to know when to be humble and when to be adamant.

God will bless those who pity the poor. This was a message to a nation that did not have a government welfare system. But there are people who do not qualify for government welfare, such as felons who have served their time in prison and have been released. Also, some companies will not hire them.

Just because you got your feelings hurt does not mean it would be wise to get revenge. Forgiveness will reduce the hurt, revenge will not.

Without wisdom, there is always a way that seems right, but it only seems right.

Do not fear Satan's fear. But it would be wise to fear God's fear.

Any preacher who is anointed with the fire of the Holy Spirit can preach scorching sermons. Those who get burned, but refuse to repent, will not speak well of the preacher.

You need to swallow your pride, or else your pride will swallow you.

Life seems so long when you are going through it; but when you are through it and look back, life seems so short.

Sometimes a young boy will want to be like his father. If you have a young son, do you want him to grow up imitating you? If not, why not?

A suspicious person is apt to create in his own mind whatever he suspects. He may believe he does not have to have proof to justify his suspicions.

Parents, pray for your children who have run away from home. They cannot outrun your prayers.

How would you feel if you saw a bumper sticker that said GOD BLESS ABORTION? Would you put such a sticker on your bumper?

When we are young and in our prime, we think we are made out of stainless steel and we will always shine. (song writers, would this not make a good song).

An idle mind is the devil's workshop.

Girls, I am sorry to say this, but you may have to kiss a lot of frogs in order to find your Prince Charming.

We are in a battle with Satan, Our mind is the battleground, and God's words are the weapons. Never fight with your own words, you will lose the battle.

Your emotions follow closely on the heels of your thinking. If you have stinking thinking, you will have stinking emotions.

When you are reading the bible, and the verse starts with "Therefore", you need to read the previous verse to see what "Therefore" is there for.

With our tongue, we praise God. With our tongue, we curse people who are made in the image of God. This is being double minded. A person who is double minded is unstable in all of his ways, according to the bible.

Say "I believe God's overwhelming love drives out overwhelming fear." If you don't yet believe it, say it over and over until you do believe it. God's word has the power to bring itself to fulfilment if we speak it often enough. A word is not a word until it is spoken, just like a song is not a song until we sing it, or at least sing it under our breath.

Where the Spirit of God is, there is wisdom. Where the spirit of God is, there is liberty. So, invite God's Spirit into your life.

You can be bold without being rude.
The truth may sound rude to some people
because they do not want to hear it.

Those who have committed themselves to
serve God have a covenant right to claim God's
blessings. However, God may bless you on his accord
if he believes he can use it to get your attention,
or due to his other servants praying for you.

Our faith is what ignites the fuse
of God's power in our lives.

Relationships between people tend to
create ties that might hinder the ties that
we need to have with God. Some refer to
the ties between people as "soul" ties.

You do not have to respond to every voice
that comes your way. Only challenge the voices
that hinder your destiny. Ignore those voices
that merely make you feel uncomfortable.

Whoever pays the fiddler has the right to
call the tunes. How does this relate to a bribe?

9

It would be wise not to get too attached to this
world. We are like a flower in the field of life.
We sprout, we grow up, we blossom, we flourish,
we fade, we wither, the wind blows us away and
the place where we stood becomes vacant.

Everyone can hear what God
has to say. He created us that way. But
some people choose not to listen.

We must always be aware of our own
thoughts. When we meditate on grudges, we are
allowing others to control our thoughts. Forgiving
others allows us to control our own thoughts.

If you can transform your thoughts,
you can transform your world, your
world, not someone else's world.

Don't tell your children what you feel
their destiny is, tell them to allow God to
reveal to them what their destiny is.

Thoughts can create pictures in our minds
and pictures create destinies, whether good or
bad. We become what we behold, what we see.

God created the first man, Adam, in such a way
that wild animals were afraid of him. Man lost this
when Adam chose to believe Satan rather than God.

Trust is a two-way street. We cannot expect
God to trust us if we do not trust him.

People talk about taking drugs that will
put them on a high. But there is no high like
the Most High, the Most High God.

Some people wish they could live their
life over. Today is the first day of the rest of
your life, what are you going to do with it?

Pride confesses other people's
sins rather its own sins.

Is there wisdom in this statement: The
primary difference between men and boys
is the amount they pay for their toys?

Why curse the dark if you can turn
on a light? Why suffer hurt if you can find
relief by forgiving those who hurt you.

If you do not know how to come to God,
ask God to come to you. Say to God, "Speak,
your servant is listening." Of course, this only
applies to those who are God's servants.

Most people's greatest fear is the fear of death,
even though they have known all of their adult
life that at some point in time death is inevitable.
Knowing this does not calm our fear of death.
Jesus said those who believe in him, trust him, and
accept him will not experience death. Death will
be like going to sleep. For this to be true, it would
have to include those who die in tragic accidents.

It may be that some fear death because
they have a sub-conscious fear of what awaits
them on the other side. This is not the case for
those whose heart is "right" with God, even
though their conduct is not always perfect.

Some people only work and strive and
make personal sacrifices to gain money or
property. Is this wise? What good would it do
you to gain the whole world if you end up losing

your soul? If your heart is "right" with God,
you will get your greatest gain in death.

Do not let your sins make you ashamed
to pray to God. He is the only one who
can remove your sins from you.

Does the following statement sound like
wisdom? You will be happier when you give than
when you receive. Put it to the test before you decide.

Some people try to destroy what
they want but cannot have.

Your soul will always be restless until
it finds rest in the one who made it.

It would be wise to set a goal to do at least
one good deed each day, even if it is a small deed.

The head of the house sets the tone for
the whole house. Jesus, being the head of his
house sets the tone for his whole house.

If you cannot be sympathetic about the
souls of your enemies, you need to start being
concerned about your own soul, because your

enemies are also made in God's image. And God
loves them just as much as he loves you.

Life is all about love, not goose bump love,
but love as described in the bible. Love that is
based on an act of our will, our determination
to love, whether we feel like it or not.

Today, if you hear God's voice, do not harden
your heart, or else you will not enter into his rest.

God opposes the proud, but
gives grace to the humble.

People can be together physically and
still not be reconciled in their minds.

A word of wisdom to all sopranos: A high
note is nothing more than a scream on pitch.

Being able to communicate with words is part of
what makes humans different from all other creatures.
The ability to communicate with words is what
connects people to God and to each other. It is obvious
from the bible that God expects people to have a high
respect for words and not misuse them or abuse them.
In the bible we see statements like this "Death and life
are in the power of the tongue. By your words you will

be justified and by your words you will be condemned. You will be held accountable for even idle (useless, barren) words." So, choose your words carefully.

Having a positive attitude comes more
easily when we have a thankful attitude.

A thankful attitude lifts the spirits of
those around us, as well as our own spirit.

In order to practice being thankful,
we have to "think" thankfulness.

People who practice being thankful continually
are pleasant to be around continually.

Do not say Thank You to a waitress at a restaurant, then leave a stingy tip. Have you ever heard the expression "Money talks?" Your tip will tell on you.

Being thankful will put
another star in your crown.

Being thankful is contagious.

Husbands, even though your wife is not perfect, look for what you can be thankful for, and tell her so. You will make her day, and yours too.

If you have a thankful heart, you
will do life with excellence.

The goal of a marriage is to become
"best" friends. You have to work on it, it does
not "just" happen. Some people have to be
kind by an act of their will, because for them
being kind is not part of their nature.

The bible teaches that when we don't have a
thankful heart, we give a place in our heart to the devil,
who is a destroyer. He is an expert in destroying peace.

God's overwhelming love casts out
overwhelming fear if we accept his love.

Beauty is in the eye of the beholder.

Most things we lose (for whatever reason)
can be replaced, but only God can make up for
lost time. He told the Israelites that he would
restore the years that the locust had eaten.

Salvation is free, but the kingdom of God is not.
You will have to fight a fight of faith to enter into
the kingdom of God, because the very foundation of
God's kingdom is faith. Even God has to have faith
in his words in order for his words to have power.

How can you enjoy life if those things you like best are either illegal, immoral or fattening? If this describes you, it is obvious that you are not spending enough time reading the bible. The more you get into God's word, the more God's word will get into you. When it gets into you in a significant amount, it will cause a "shift" in your thinking. As a man thinks in his heart so is he, according to the bible. It is impossible to think crooked and live straight.

We are born with the birth mark of Satan on us. We inherited it from Adam, who received it from Satan when he decided to believe Satan rather than God.

The birth mark is not physically visible, and it involves fear.

When you read the bible regularly, you honor God, because God's word is God. You cannot honor God at a distance.

Patience is a virtue. An absence of patience genders strife, and causes accidents.

If you take a good look at yourself, you may begin to see other people differently.

If you harbor a grudge, you
will never experience peace.

If you put your trust in God, and
tell him so, he can make a way for you
when there seems to be no way.

Fill your heart with God's word before a
crisis comes. Noah did not wait until it started
to rain before he started building the Ark.

God has promised he will keep in
perfect peace those whose minds are focused
on him. How can you focus on someone you
cannot see? Focus on God's word as recorded
in the bible, because God's word is God.

Everyone has a mission in life that God
wants them to fulfil, but God cannot reveal to
us what our mission is if we are too occupied
following our own personal mission, which
includes our own personal religion.

The primary battle is not between people and
Satan. The primary battle is between God and Satan,
and the prize that goes to the winner is people. It
is God's desire that no person will go to hell. It is
Satan's desire that no person will go to heaven.

If you are God's servant, you can decree a thing. Say, "As Jesus is so am I in this world." You can also decree it for your family. Insert their name for "I" in the decree. It can be used to address health issues, fear, addictions, deliverance from demons, etc.

God is the author of true wisdom, not worldly wisdom.

It is difficult to deal with a rebel because he is in love with himself, or else he goes to the other extreme and hates himself. God's words will address both extremes.

The best way to destroy your enemy is to make him your friend. If he is hungry, feed him. If he is sick, heal him. If he is deaf, open his ears. If he is blind, restore his sight. If he crucifies you, forgive him. (you will need God's help on this).

The pleasures of sin will not outweigh the regrets that will come later.

Man's limitations are God's opportunities.

A question of wisdom: Are church steeples any different from the Tower of Babel? Read Genesis 11:4 and notice the words "let us make a name".

Our disqualifications qualify us for God's grace. If we were perfect, we would not need God's grace.

Spoken godly words, spoken in obedience rather faith, will have the same results as words spoken in faith. Can you see how important obedience is? Speaking God's words in obedience produces faith.

When you are under so much pressure that you are unable to pray about your situation, ask Jesus to pray for you. It is scriptural to ask this of Jesus.

Angel's are listening for our words that give voice to God's words, according to Psalms 103:20. This verse says the angels "do God's commandments" that we voice. When our voice is idle, the angels are idle.

What we focus on intently we empower to have power in our thinking, whether for good or for bad.

God honors those who honor him. He will elevate those that elevate him. He will acknowledge those who acknowledge him.

We will need wisdom to know whether we are worshipping God or religion, which has a form of godliness, and some are deceived by it.

Some people are willing to serve
God, but only as an advisor.

Could this be considered words of
wisdom: You are more apt to find God
when you come to the end of yourself?

Church members, if you want a better pastor,
pray diligently for the one you already have. There is a
strong possibility that he will become a better pastor.

Unfortunately, some people's favorite jam is
made from forbidden fruit. Read Genesis 3:1-3.

Notice how you react to people. This
will tell you if you are allowing them to
control your thoughts and actions.

Preachers, if you change God's message,
God's message will not change the people.

When you pray or just talk to God, do not be
concerned if your words are not eloquent. Remember,
God looks on the heart in addition to listening
to our words. He hears the cry of our heart.

Fathers, raising your children will be a lot of trouble to you, but they are worth it. And in your old age, they will be available to "raise" you.

If the devil does not harass you, it is probably because you are no threat to his kingdom. Read your bible more, and be diligent to do what it says, then you will be a threat to his kingdom. Then he will harass you.

Your desperation is God's opportunity to help you if you cooperate with him.

If we combine our faith with someone who has faith, the power of our faith is multiplied. If one can chase a thousand, two can chase ten thousand.

Be forewarned that if you have made a commitment to serve God, you will encounter opposition from the devil, whose strategy is to deceive you. He is a professional deceiver. If he is not successful with deception, his next weapon will be fear.

If we put our faith in creation rather than God, we fall from God's grace and redemption.

Talk to God about your visions and dreams for your future. He is just as interested in them as you are.

You can predict your future by noticing what type of people you hang around with during your free time.

When you have a genuine encounter with Jesus, you will not talk to him about yourself. If you are now spending a lot of your time talking about others, that is proof that you have not had a genuine encounter with Jesus.

When you are diligent to do what God has asked you to do, he is responsible for the results. Noah preached for 120 years while he built the Ark, and never won a single convert, other than his family.

When life gets complicated and you are tempted to quit whatever God has called you to do, remove from your mind the thoughts of quitting. Then life will become less complicated.

Our goal in life is to be so full of God's power that the devil is more afraid of us than we are of him.

The bible says, "Seek first the kingdom of God." It does not say, seek first the church. You can be in church and still not be in the kingdom of God. God's kingdom can best be understood by reading Acts 2:1-39.

It would be an act of wisdom on our part if we would accept the fact that this world is not our home, our eternal home. Our eternal home is either heaven or the Lake of Fire, usually referred to as hell.

Everyone needs to spend some time thinking about, and getting ready for, our next life.

Many people have probably heard the expression "Day of Judgment". Your day of judgment will come when you fully comprehend God's words concerning life and death. Your own words to accept or reject God's words will be your "Judge". In other words, your judgment will come out of your own mouth. Read John 3:16-18 and notice the word "already" in the King James Version of the bible.

Since we do not find it among other creatures that God created, we could conclude that God wired people in the beginning to have a nature that desires to worship. This nature becomes perverted due to Adam and Eve choosing to replace God with Satan, perverted but not eliminated. We still have the nature that causes us to desire to worship, but we might choose different words to describe it. We may use the words "idolize" or "hero" or "favorite" or "like" or "cherish" or "love", etc. The object of our worship can be anything: a person, beauty, knowledge, money, animals, birds, the environment, ourselves, the true God, a false god, pride, the sun, the moon, etc. God, being a wise God, would obviously want the creature that he created in his own image to worship him. To do this, God would have to wire the creature is such a way as to have a desire to worship, even if the creature chose to worship someone or something rather than God. We have the power to choose. God did not make us robots.

10

Wisdom includes things that are practical.
Teach your young children this rhyme: Stop,
look and listen before you cross the street. Use
your eyes and ears before you use your feet.

It is not only important to know who we are,
it is also important to know who we are not.

When you are sure you have done your best, you
can find rest even if you do not succeed in what you
tried. Noah preached for 120 years, but never won a
single convert. Yet, God saved him from the flood.

You would be wise if you believed this: the
weaker sex is actually the stronger sex, because of the
weakness of the stronger sex for the weaker sex.

As you travel through life, resist the temptation to keep looking in the rearview mirror, neither for the good experiences or the bad experiences. Hope is big with God, but it only pertains to what is up ahead.

In God's language, there is no such word as "cope", but there is such a word as "hope".

In the Hebrew language, the root word for "hope is the same root word for "rope". What does that tell you?

God is not just a gift giver, he is a good gift giver.

Hate knows no fulfilment. If he kills and buries the person he hates, he has an overwhelming desire to dig him up and kill him again, hoping he will find fulfilment.

God wants to be intimately involved in our lives so he can talk to us as a friend would talk to a friend.

Fear is evil. It is of the devil. Adam and Eve were never fearful until they decided to believe the devil rather than God.

Men, I don't want to discourage you, but don't choose a girl to marry based solely

on beauty. Get to know her heart. Is it the
type of heart you are looking for?

When we surrender to Satan, we give.
When we surrender to God, we get.

God is love, so the portion of the bible that
records God's voice is his love letter to us.

If we get hurt by people's words, we
are apt to hurt others with our words.

Broken crayons can still be used to draw beautiful
pictures. How does this relate to a broken life?

Every day in God's presence is a
good day even if "things" go wrong.

In the Hebrew language there is no word for
the English word "coincidence". This has great
implications if God designed the Hebrew language.

If there is no word in the Hebrew language
for the English word "cope", it is obvious from
the bible that God expects his followers to be
overcomers, not just cope with problems.

Don't correct people using incorrect
biblical protocol. Speak the truth in love.

Having pride is like having bad
breath. Everyone knows it but you.

Does a bird sing because he has the answers
to all his problems, or does he sing because he
has a song in his heart? What about us?

A well-balanced man can laugh at himself
when he accidentally does something foolish.

If anyone offers you a breath mint, take it.

The world's Golden Rule: Whoever
has the gold makes the rules.

Ignorance is not bliss.

Might does not make right.
Might only makes might.

If you play with fire, you are apt
to get burned. Jealousy is a fire.

Adults, it would be wise to know that some
young person is watching you and listening to

you talk. They may want to imitate you, whether
for something good or something bad.

The wise will be able to keep their
minds when everyone else is losing theirs.

Sometimes the elderly are so pessimistic
about life they will not buy green bananas.
They think it is a risky investment.

To be wise, put your faith in what Jesus
did for you during his earthly ministry.

God expects his followers to be like sheep,
but it is risky to be a sheep in a world full of
wolves unless we have a brave shepherd.

For a married couple to become good
lovers they will have to become good tolerators,
because there will always be things about your
partner that you will have to tolerate.

We don't have to earn God's love, we
just have to be available to receive it.

An honoured vow has power.

If you believe your mission in life is
to fix everybody, start with yourself.

You are not responsible for the way people treat
you, but you are responsible for the way you react.

If you want to continue to rock
and roll in your old age, you will need to
put wheels on your rocking chair.

Epilogue

This book includes God's wisdom and the world's wisdom, but the primary purpose for the book is to exalt God and his wisdom. In the course of writing this book, I heard these from God, "Your pen is your pulpit." So, I took very seriously what I wrote in this book.

I hope you take these WORDS OF WISDOM seriously also. My hope is that you will grab these words of wisdom and run with them.

The bible compares speaking words to sowing seeds.

In the parable of the sower in the bible, we are apt to focus on the type of ground mentioned, but notice the sower (Jesus) sowed good seed in all types of ground. So, our job as sowers is to sow seed in all types of ground. We cannot tell in advance which soil will respond to the seeds sown.

Remember, just because a person has ears does not mean he has ears that are willing to hear. But we have to assume everyone has a hearing ear, and continue to sow seeds.

The words of wisdom in this book are only a portion of the wisdom you will receive from reading the bible for yourself. I strongly urge you to set aside a minimum of thirty minutes of your day to read the bible. To do this, you will probably have to forsake one of your favorite TV shows, but it will be worth it. Try it for one month and then you will know if it is worth it.

If you are new at reading the bible, I suggest that you start with the book called JOHN. Then read the books of MATTHEW and MARK and LUKE. These four books cover the era of Jesus' ministry while he was on the earth.

Jesus is the grand subject of the NEW TESTAMENT portion of the bible, so concentrate your bible study primarily on the NEW TESTAMENT. However, wait on studying the book called REVELATION until you are well established in the other scriptures.

I have written a book that explains the book in the bible called REVELATION. The title of the book I wrote is THE BOOK OF REVELATION FROM ALPHA TO OMEGA. You should be able to find it wherever books are sold. If you don't find it on a shelf, ask them to order it for you.

www.ingramcontent.com/pod-product-compliance
Ingram Content Group UK Ltd.
Pitfield, Milton Keynes, MK11 3LW, UK
UKHW022209230426
12048UKWH00016BA/734